Our Organic Garden

Precious McKenzie

ROURKE
PUBLISHING

www.rourkepublishing.com

www.rourkepublishing.com

PHOTO CREDITS: Cover © Chris Price; Title Page © Marek Mnich; Page 4 © Eduard Titov; Page 5 © audaxl; Page 6 © Mike Rodriguez; Page 7 © Mustafanc; Page 8, 16 © Alan Crawford; Page 9 © Alessandrozocc; Page 10 © George Clerk; Page 11 © rossariorossario, Bradcalkins; Page 12 © Dleonis; Page 13 © Dleonis, vtorous; Page 14 © Driada; Page 15 © Leonid Yakutin; Page 17 © Monkey Business Images; Page 18 © Renee Brady, ferhat mat; Page 19 © craftvision, imagedepotpro; Page 21 © Jani Bryson.

Edited by Meg Greve

Cover and Interior design by Tara Raymo

Library of Congress Cataloging-in-Publication Data

McKenzie, Precious
 Our Organic Garden / Precious McKenzie.
    p. cm. -- (Green Earth Science Discovery Library)
 Includes bibliographical references and index.
 ISBN 978-1-61741-767-2 (hard cover) (alk. paper)
 ISBN 978-1-61741-969-0 (soft cover)
 Library of Congress Control Number: 2011924813

Rourke Publishing
Printed in the United States of America, North Mankato, Minnesota
060711
060711CL

www.rourkepublishing.com - rourke@rourkepublishing.com
Post Office Box 643328 Vero Beach, Florida 32964

Table of Contents

Want to be a Gardener?

Do you want to grow your own food?
Do you want to help make the world a
little cleaner?

Then you should try **organic** gardening!

Why Organic?

Organic gardeners grow fruits and vegetables without using harmful **chemicals**. This means they don't use man-made fertilizers or **pesticides**.

Organic gardeners use natural methods to help their crops grow. They do not want to **pollute** the Earth or the water.

compost bin

Organic gardeners use **compost** and **manure** to keep their soil healthy.

Aphids can destroy a garden.
Ladybugs love to eat aphids!

They use helpful insects to keep the
harmful insects away.

Let's Get Started

You do not need a lot of space to start your own garden.

First, till the soil. Remove rocks and roots.

Measure rows for your seeds.

Spread a layer of compost or manure.

Plant the seeds in the soil. Cover the seeds with a light layer of soil.

Now watch your garden grow!

Sprinkle the soil with water.

Pull weeds that could get in the way of your plants.

Check your garden every day.

Water the soil if it looks too dry. Look out for insects and other creatures that might eat all of your plants.

Organic products do not contain poisons or chemicals. Organic foods are safer for people to eat.

Organic gardeners reuse soil, leaves, and roots as compost for the next season's crop.

Organic gardeners love to eat the food they grow. They take pride in knowing that they did not pollute the Earth or water supply by their farming.

Gardening Tips

Each type of plant is different. Some plants grow best in dry **climates**. Others grow best in very moist climates.

Read the labels on seed packages to find the plants that grow best in your climate zone.

Some plants need lots of sunlight. Others
need some shade.

Gardening is a lot of work and a lot of fun. Ask friends and family to help you grow your organic garden. Share the food you grow!

Try This

You can make a mini compost pile in your garden. It may take a couple of months, but the healthy soil you get will be worth the wait!

1. Find an empty spot in your garden or backyard.
2. Dig a hole that is about 18 inches (46 centimeters) deep.
3. Fill the hole with fruit or vegetable scraps, dead leaves, and coffee grounds.
4. Cover the hole with a layer of dirt.
5. Wait one to two months. Dig up the compost and sprinkle it in your garden, or grow a plant right in the hole!

WARNING!

Do not use dairy or meat in your compost hole. Critters will try to dig it up and eat it!

Glossary

chemicals (KEM-uh-kuhls): substances that are used in science and manufacturing that can be harmful when not used carefully

climates (KLYE-mits): places where the weather is usually the same

compost (KOM-pohst): a mixture of dead leaves, vegetables, and coffee grounds that is used to make soil healthy for growing

manure (muh-NOO-ur): animal waste used in gardening soil

organic (or-GAN-ik): made of only natural materials

pesticides (PES-tu-sides): chemicals used to kill insects or other creatures who eat plants in gardens

pollute (puh-LOOT): to make air, water, or soil dirty using trash or chemicals

Index

Websites

About the Author

Precious McKenzie lives in Florida with her husband, three children, and two dogs. She writes books for children and teaches English at the University of South Florida. In her free time, she enjoys horseback riding.